DEMCO

A fashionable HISTORY of MAKEUP & BODY DECORATION

Raintree

A FASHIONABLE HISTORY OF MAKEUP &
BODY DECORATION
was produced by

David West 👫 **Children's Books**
7 Princeton Court
55 Felsham Road
London SW15 1AZ

This edition first published in the United Sates in
2003 by Raintree, a division of Reed Elsevier, Inc.,
Chicago, Illinois.

For information address the publishers:
Raintree
100 N. LaSalle
Suite 1200
Chicago, IL 60602

Author: Helen Reynolds
Editors: Jackie Gaff, Marta Segal Block
Picture Research: Carlotta Cooper
Designer: Julie Joubinaux

Library of Congress Cataloging-in-Publication Data:
Reynolds, Helen, 1956-
  Makeup and body decoration / Helen Reynolds.
    p. cm. -- (Fashionable history of costume)
Summary: A brief history of makeup and other forms of body
decoration,
from false eyebrows made of mouse skins to fake tans.
Includes bibliographical references and index.
  ISBN 1-4109-0028-2 (lib. bdg.)
  1. Cosmetics--Juvenile literature. 2. Body marking--Juvenile
literature. [1. Cosmetics. 2. Beauty, Personal.] I. Title. II. Series.
  GT2340.R49 2003
  391.6'3--dc21
                          2002153950

ISBN 1-4109-0028-2

07 06 05 04 03
10 9 8 7 6 5 4 3 2 1

PHOTO CREDITS:

Abbreviations: t-top, m-middle, b-bottom, r-right,
l-left, c-center.

The publisher would like to thank the following for
permission to reproduce photographs:
Front cover m & 10l, tl &12bl, r & 18l and pages,
5tr, 6br, 10br, 11tr, 12tl & r, 16tr, 17tl & tr, 20-21,
23l, 24tl, 25r & 26bl – Mary Evans Picture
Library; pages 3, 4br, 5br, 6-7t, 16bl, 19bl, 24tr &
b, 25tl – Dover Books; pages 4tr, 6tl & bl 9tr, 22br,
26r, 28bl, 29r & b – The Culture Archive; pages
5l, 7 all, 8 ml, 9bl & br, 11tl & br, 13tl & br, 14l
& tr, 15tl & br, 17bl, 18tr, 19tr & br, 20tr, 21 &
br, 22bl, 23br, 25 bl, 27tr & br, 28-29 – Rex
Features Ltd; page 8tl – The Kobal
Collection/BFI/United Artists; pages 14-15 – The
Kobal Collection/ICON/Ladd Co./Paramount; page
8bl – Hulton Archive; page 11b – Corbis Images;
pages 13tr, 27l – Digital Stock; page 20tl –
ISG113867 A Young Lady of Fashion (oil on panel)
by Paolo Uccello (1397-1475), Isabella Stewart
Gardner Museum, Boston, Massachusetts,
USA/Bridgeman Art Library; page
22tr – (LDBDA s236 – Elephant ivory dentures
featuring human, or "Waterloo" teeth, and human
teeth strung together for sale, 1815-1820) and m
(LDBDA s301 – "A French dentist shewing a
specimen of his artificial teeth and false palates,"
1785, Thomas Rowlandson [caricaturing Nicholas
Dubois de Chémant]/British Dental Association
Museum Collection).

Printed and bound in China

A fashionable HISTORY *of* MAKEUP & BODY DECORATION

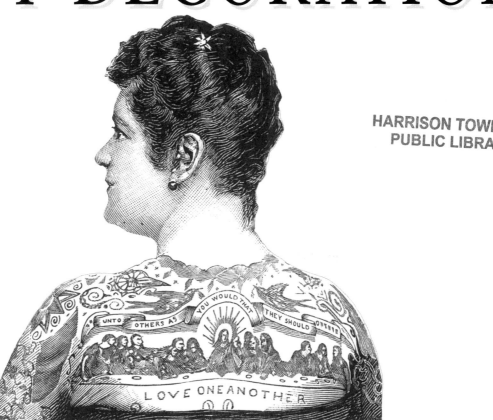

Contents

ANCIENT ADORNMENT

Women and men were beautifying themselves with makeup back in ancient Egyptian times.

MAKING A LASTING IMPRESSION

Although the tattooist's art is at least 5,000 years old, its revived popularity in the West dates from the 1760s. Illustrated men and women with the kind of allover tattoo shown below were popular exhibits at fairgrounds and circuses in the early 19th century.

From Eye Paint to Illustrated Skin

A stroll down a busy street in any of the world's major cities will reveal countless variations in face and body decoration. Most people now take the freedom to experiment with their appearance for granted. The presence or absence of makeup is widely accepted, as are tattoos and body piercing. Body decoration is not a modern phenomenon, however, and it has meant different things in different cultures throughout history. Among other things, certain forms of makeup can symbolize social status or proclaim membership in a group. Above all, though, makeup has been used to enhance beauty, with every era setting its own standard of fashionable perfection.

Makeup for the Masses

In the 1920s mass production made cosmetics more widely available.

Cutting a Fine Figure

Fashions in facial hair have fluctuated over the years. In the early 1900s, the stylish swell sported a big, bushy moustache.

Homemade Beauty Aids

Caring for the skin has always been as important as covering it up with makeup. Recipes that use kitchen ingredients to whip up face masks and skin ointments have been around since ancient times.

The Eyes Have It

Eye paints date back to antiquity and originally may have been used as a form of magical eye protection. By ancient Egyptian times, however, vanity had taken over and eye makeup was used by both men and women as a beauty aid.

Mice in the makeup box

Ideas about eye beauty changed over the centuries, with some strange practices coming and going. In the 18th century, fashionable women shaved off their eyebrows and applied artificial ones made from a mouse's skin!

EGYPTIAN BEAUTY SECRETS

Egyptians used powdered minerals in their eye makeup. Eyes were either outlined in kohl, made from black galena (a lead ore) or with green malachite (a copper ore).

ELIZABETHAN EYESORE

Queen Elizabeth I (above, 1533–1603) used drops of the poisonous deadly nightshade plant (below) to make her pupils larger and her eyes appear brighter. Fashionable women continued this practice for centuries afterward.

NEW TAKE ON AN OLD LOOK

This magazine feature illustrated the 1960s fashion for Egyptian-style eye makeup.

Victorian modesty gives way to flapper flamboyance

By the 19th century makeup was frowned upon and it was only worn in an obvious way by the kind of women considered disreputable, such as actresses and prostitutes. The early 20th century saw huge changes in women's lives, however, and an accompanying shakeup in acceptable behavior.

The short hair and cloche hats of the 1920s flapper girl drew attention to the face. Eyes were highlighted with an eyebrow pencil and colored eyeshadow, as well as plenty of dark mascara to darken the lashes. In the following decades the emphasis was more on the lips, but as skirts shrank in the 1960s, eyes became big again—literally. Young women made their eyes look bigger with opalescent eye shadow, false eyelashes, and thick, black eyeliner.

CUSTOMIZED CONTACT

Contact lenses with colors and patterns were introduced in the late 20th century as a new way to emphasize the eyes.

MODEL MAKEUP

With her dark, heavily made-up eyes, pale lips, and short, geometric haircut, the fashion model Twiggy (Leslie Hornby, 1949–) was the epitome of 1960s glamour.

LUSH LASHES

Although at their most popular in the 1960s and 1970s, false eyelashes have been around since the early 1900s.

Painted Men

In the 18th century, upper-class men and women wore elaborate makeup, including lip paints made from colored plaster of paris.

Lovely Lips

Lip paint is another beauty aid that dates back to ancient times. Neatly packaged lipsticks weren't available in those days, of course, and cosmetics were made by the wearer or a servant. The ancient Egyptians ground up a mineral called red ochre, while the Greeks mashed up seaweed and mulberries.

Nature & artifice

Bold use of lip paint has gone in and out of vogue over the years. Roman women loved bright lips, for example, while in the Middle Ages a more natural look was preferred.

In 17th- and 18th-century Europe, lip paints were used by the nobility of both sexes, as a mark of their social rank. After the French Revolution, however, Europe was swept by a new passion for simplicity in clothing and general appearance. Men stopped wearing lip paint, and there was a sharp decline in its use by women that continued throughout much of the Victorian era.

Pretty Boys

The 1980s saw a general trend toward glitz and glamour. In subcultures such as the New Romantics, men and women wore heavy makeup, including dramatic lipstick.

Lip Stuff

The twist-up lipstick in a metal tube was a 20th-century invention. Before then, lip paint mainly came in little pots and was applied with the finger or a brush.

Seeing Red

Although during much of the 19th century makeup was frowned upon, from the 1890s onward, suffragettes campaigning for votes for women sometimes adopted red lip paint. It was a symbol of their defiance of traditional ideas about acceptable female behavior.

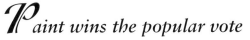

Paint wins the popular vote

By the early 20th century, discreet lip paint was again being used by society ladies. Lip crayons had been around since the 16th century, but most lip paints came in pots, were greasy, and needed a skillful hand to apply them. In 1915 the first lipstick in a sliding metal tube was patented. This easy-to-apply product was an immediate success and was soon being manufactured in a range of red tints. By the 1920s the wearing of lipstick was commonplace among stylish women, and has remained so until the present day.

Red for victory

New clothes were in short supply during World War II (1939–1945), so women used makeup to boost morale and add glamour to their lives.

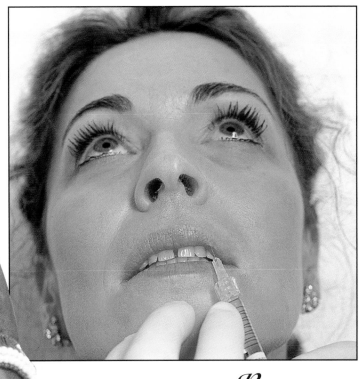

Big is beautiful

Lip paint isn't the only way of drawing attention to the lips. In some cultures (left), huge plugs are used to stretch them. In others (above), people have their lips injected with a substance called collagen.

The Painted Face

In the Western world up until the early 20th century, pale skin was a sign of wealth and status. Suntans were abhorred because they were associated with outdoor work and lower status. The wealthy painted and powdered their faces the palest shades of white.

Fashion victims

Smallpox was commonplace until a vaccine for the disease was perfected in the late 1790s, and face makeup allowed victims to cover spots and scars.

Recipes for whitening the skin and hiding blemishes have been around since Roman times. Although some ingredients were harmless, others such as powdered white lead were definitely dangerous. Mild lead poisoning caused headaches, nausea, and stomach cramps. The worst cases ended in insanity, paralysis, or death.

EAST MEETS WEST

White face makeup has also been worn by nonwhite cultures. White rice powder is part of the traditional makeup of the Japanese geisha.

ELIZABETHAN ELEGANCE

Like other noblewomen of her day, Elizabeth I whitened her face with a thick layer of toxic, lead-based paint.

Masked beauty

Early 20th-century cosmetics such as Max Factor's Pan-Cake brand coated the skin and created a rather masklike effect. The skin tones were naturalistic, but the end result was almost as artificial as the white face paint of earlier eras.

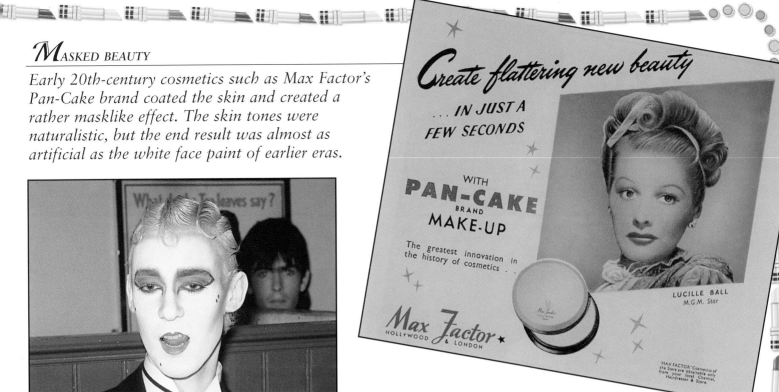

Create flattering new beauty

...IN JUST A FEW SECONDS

WITH PAN-CAKE BRAND MAKE-UP

The greatest innovation in the history of cosmetics...

Max Factor ★
HOLLYWOOD & LONDON

LUCILLE BALL
M.G.M. Star

'MAX FACTOR' Cosmetics of the Stars are obtainable only from your local Chemist, Hairdresser & Store.

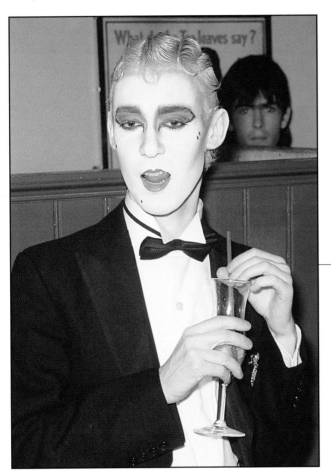

Ghostly white

Although flesh-toned makeup has dominated fashion since the early 20th century, the unnaturally white-faced look has sometimes resurfaced, such as this look of the 1980s.

Ending the coverup

When makeup fell from favor in the 19th century, the use of harmful products such as white lead declined. When makeup came back in vogue in the early 20th century, a more natural look was in and women began wearing flesh-toned cosmetics. Early foundations and powders still tended to cover up the skin, creating a thick, matte (non-shiny) surface. It wasn't until the 1980s that sheerer, more light-reflective products became available.

Painted warriors

Face paints have long been used in war—either as a very visible message of identity (above) or to camouflage soldiers (left), helping them blend into the background.

Finishing Touches

Today we use blush to give cheeks a rosy glow. In the 17th and 18th centuries, the nobility smeared on a red paste called rouge, creating a look that to modern eyes appears more feverish than healthy.

Cheery cheeks

No 18th-century lady's makeup was complete without a liberal application of rouge.

Patching over the cracks

Smallpox scars and other blemishes were hidden beneath black patches designed to look like natural beauty spots. In 18th-century Britain, patches were also used by the nobility to indicate which political party they supported. Tories wore patches on their left cheeks, while the Whigs wore them on their right.

Desperate measures

To achieve a fashionable pallor, some Victorian ladies resorted to having themselves injected with dangerous substances peddled by quack chemists.

A passion for patches

Originally used to cover blemishes, beauty patches became more elaborate in the 18th century, and were cut into stars, hearts, and other shapes.

HOLY MARK

In countries such as India, it is traditional for Hindus to make a colored mark on the forehead as a sign of piety. In the past, married women often wore red marks, while unmarried ones had black marks. Today, the marks often match the color of the woman's sari.

PUNK PATTERNING

In the 1970s, punk rockers took the art of face decoration to new extremes, using everything from paints to piercings.

NATURAL BEAUTY

In the 1950s, women used eyebrow pencils to copy the natural beauty spots of film stars like Marilyn Monroe (left, 1926–1962).

From pallor to perfection

By the 1790s the passion for patches was fading, and only older women and actresses continued to apply rouge. For much of the 19th century it was fashionable for ladies to look "pale and interesting," with only a slight pink tinge in the cheeks— a state that was induced by avoiding fresh air and by dubious practices such as drinking vinegar.

The revived popularity of makeup in the early 20th century was accompanied by a renewed interest in rouge, which was now considerably lighter in both color and consistency, and often came in powdered form.

Painted Bodies

Like cave art, body painting was probably among the earliest form of human artistic expression. It was practiced by a diverse range of cultures and on most continents, from the Americas to Australia. We cannot be certain why prehistoric people developed this art, but one reason may have been to mark momentous occasions in life.

ALL DRESSED UP

In some cultures body paint is seen as a form of clothing— people would feel naked without it.

TIMELESS TRADITION

Body art has deep spiritual significance for the aboriginal peoples of Australia, and many communities have their own unique patterns.

Rites of passage

Body art may have been used to mark a person's death and departure to the afterlife, for example, or to give symbolic protection when undertaking a difficult hunt or journey. Traditionally, the paints were made from berries, bark, leaves, and minerals such as red and yellow ochre, which were ground up and then mixed with vegetable oils or animal fat.

Youth Protest

In the 1960s, some young people used body paint in order to differentiate themselves from mainstream Western society.

Art & society

In some cultures people have used body art as an important means of setting themselves apart from animals. It has also served to indicate social rank, and to distinguish one tribe from another.

Other cultures have practiced body art for different reasons. Face painting has long been an essential part of the circus clown's art, for instance, and performance artists often use the body as a canvas. For children, having the face painted like an animal or a pirate is just part of the fun of dressing up, and face-painting stalls are now a frequent sight at parties and malls.

Blue Streak

The Celtic peoples of ancient Britain made a blue body paint from the leaves of the woad plant, a kind of mustard. They used it to make themselves look even more terrifying in battle, as seen on Mel Gibson in Braveheart (1995).

Pretty Palms

In India (right) and North Africa, the plant dye henna has been used for centuries to create elaborate body art for weddings and other ceremonies. Henna is now often used for temporary tattoos.

Body Scarring & Piercing

More permanent than body painting, scarring and piercing have also been practiced for centuries. The reasons for these body arts vary among cultures, and are often related to social rank or rites of passage.

Making a lasting impression

Scarring techniques differed, but they often involved scratching patterns into the skin with a sharp object such as a stone or a shell. An irritant such as wood ash was then rubbed into the cuts, leaving behind raised bumps and ridges after the skin healed.

Marked man

Although rarely done today, body scarring was traditional among aboriginal Australians.

Taking a piercing interest

Body piercing is far more widespread than scarring, and it has been done on virtually every part of the body. Through the pierced holes, ornaments made from metal, bone, shell, or glass are inserted. Lip plugs were worn by the Maya of ancient Mexico and the Inuit of Alaska. Nose rings have long been traditional in India, Pakistan, and many other countries.

Nosing around

Piercing the septum, or center of the nose, was most common among warrior cultures. Nose plugs can be almost an inch thick.

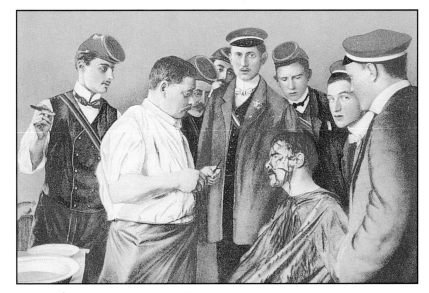

Battle scars

Until the beginning of the 20th century, German university students settled quarrels by fighting sword duels. Dueling scars were considered manly and were worn with pride.

Social stigma

From ancient times to the early 19th century, branding scars were used in Europe to set criminals apart from the rest of society.

Anything goes

In mainstream fashion over the past few hundred years, the ears have been the most commonly pierced body part. It's no surprise, then, that people reacted with shocked horror when punk rockers began piercing other body parts with safety pins in the 1970s. The shock didn't last long, however, and nose, eyebrow, lip, tongue, and navel piercing is now widely accepted—and widely practiced by young people everywhere.

Taking a tip from ancient history

When people took up multiple ear-piercing, in the 1980s, they revived a practice that has been around for 4,000 years.

Trendy Tattoos

Tattooing is another permanent form of body art, a cross between painting and scarring. Patterns are made by pricking tiny holes, through which colored pigments seep into the skin. In the past, tattoos were done by hand, using a sharp stick, bone, or needle. In the early 1890s, the practice was revolutionized by the invention of the electric tattoo machine.

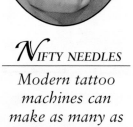

NIFTY NEEDLES
Modern tattoo machines can make as many as 3,000 tiny holes per minute.

Icemen & mummies

Like other forms of body art, tattoos have been used in different ways by different cultures. Sometimes purely to decorate the body, other times to communicate social status. One of the oldest known examples of tattooed skin was found on the body of Utzi the Iceman, who died more than 5,200 years ago in the mountains between Italy and Austria. Tattoos have also been discovered on 4,000-year-old Egyptian mummies.

THE ART OF THE JAPANESE TATTOOIST

In Japan, tattooing began to flourish as an art form in the 18th century. Inspiration for the elaborate images came from woodcuts and watercolors.

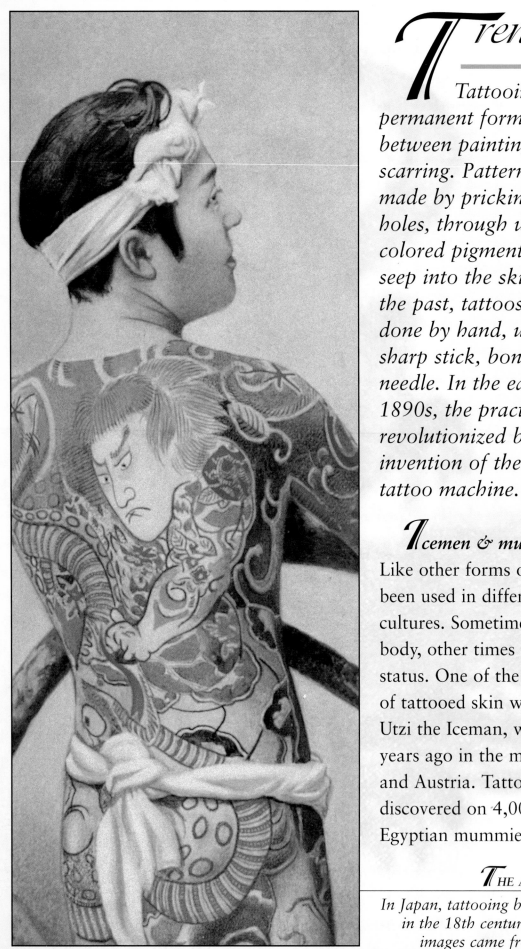

Temporary tattoos

Henna is not the only form of temporary tattoo. Stick-on tattoos are also available. They usually last for one to two weeks.

Sailors

In the West, interest in tattoos was revived by the voyages of Captain James Cook (1728–1779) into the Pacific during the 1760s and 1770s. Fascinated by the customs of the Pacific Islanders, some of Cook's crew were themselves tattooed, which started a trend among sailors. Tattooing is now seen as a highly skilled art form, particularly as practiced in Japan and by the Maoris of New Zealand.

Maori messages

Called Ta Moko, the traditional Maori tattoo records family history as well as tribal status.

Step right up

Although common among Western sailors by the early 19th century, tattoos were seen as highly exotic by most landlubbers. Tattooed women and men were a popular exhibit at fairgrounds and circuses, and people paid money to gasp and stare.

Preparation makes perfect

Modern tattooists usually plan complex designs on paper first. Using a stencil, the design is then tranferred to the skin to guide the tattoo needle.

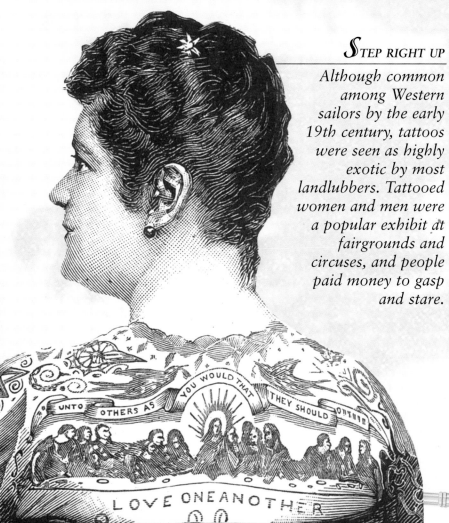

UNTO OTHERS AS YOU WOULD THAT THEY SHOULD UNTO

LOVE ONEANOTHER

High Society

During the 15th century, European noblewomen shaved their hair and sometimes their eyebrows to achieve a fashionably high forehead.

In each culture and era, people have had different ideas about beauty. In the West in the late 19th century, for instance, women used corsets and bottom-enlarging bustles to create voluptuous S-shaped curves. In the 1920s and 1960s, the stylish woman's figure was boyishly flat-chested.

Bound head & foot

In some cultures, the pursuit of the perfect body shape led to more drastic actions. Until the custom was banned in 1911, young girls in well-to-do Chinese families had their feet bound to restrict their growth. In some African and North American communities, the practice of head shaping dates back hundreds of years.

Head start

In the past, the Chinook people of northwestern North America practiced head-shaping by strapping their children's heads between wooden planks.

Neck bands

Among the Padaung tribe of Myanmar, an elongated neck is considered beautiful for women. Gold or copper neck-rings are added over a period of time to stretch the neck.

While some people spend their lives dieting to reduce their body size, others spend most of their time exercising to increase it. Body builders treat their bodies like a living sculpture, building up muscle strength and size through weight training and special diets.

*N*ipping & tucking

Today, the craft of the plastic surgeon has far outpaced ancient body shaping techniques. It is now possible for people to have virtually every part of their body altered. Excess fat can be removed through a technique called liposuction, breasts are enlarged, entire faces are reshaped, and wrinkles treated with chemical injections. Despite known risks and extremely high costs of such procedures, an increasing number of women and men are regularly submitting their bodies to the scalpel, all in search of the appearance of youth.

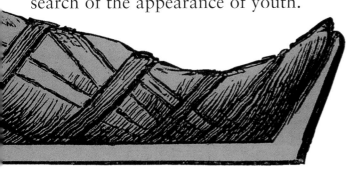

*B*EAUTY AT ANY PRICE

Like many stars, the singer and actress Cher (1946–) has undergone many plastic surgeries, having her face "lifted" and other areas reshaped.

Tooth & Nail

Many a beauty's smile was marred by rotten or missing teeth before the 19th century, when modern dental science began to develop and people began to understand the causes of tooth decay. In the past, the cheapest solution was to have rotten teeth extracted—an excruciatingly painful business before anesthetics were invented in the 1840s.

Teething problems

The first known sets of false teeth were made in Italy around 2,700 years ago, by the Etruscans. The use of dentures had died out by the Middle Ages, however, and when they were reintroduced in the 17th century, only the wealthy could afford them. More ornamental than practical, early dentures often fell out and had to be removed for eating.

What a Mouthful

Early false teeth were carved from animal bone, ivory, or mother-of-pearl, or cast in silver or gold. Human teeth were also used, either pulled from the dead or sold by poor people from their own mouths.

Cultural differences

Not everyone thinks that even, glistening white teeth are beautiful. In parts of Africa and Southeast Asia, teeth are filed into sharp points or dyed different colors.

Mouth jewelry

Decorating teeth with precious jewels is not a new custom. Hundreds of years ago, the Mayan people of South America inlaid their teeth with turquoise and jade.

LADIES OF LEISURE

In China, it was once the custom for noblewomen to grow their nails more than 9 inches (25 centimeters) long. Sometimes the nails were sheathed in gold or silver to protect them.

Hands-on experience

Throughout history, clean hands and buffed, filed fingernails have been considered a sign of the leisured upper classes. At times it was also fashionable for the aristocracy to show that they didn't need to work by growing extremely long nails, clearly unsuitable for manual labor.

Nail polish didn't come on the market until the mid-1920s, when it was sold with the new, mass-produced makeup. Open-toed sandals became fashionable at this time, and women started to paint their toenails. In the 1930s, it became stylish to coordinate nail polish and lipstick colors.

The 1980s was the age of power dressing, and no career women looked complete without immaculate nails. Once a service offered only by hair salons, manicures could now be had in nail salons that sprouted up everywhere.

FAKING FINE FINGERNAILS

Although artificial nails didn't become a fashion accessory until the 1970s, they were marketed to nail biters as early as the 1930s. These days they're available in a range of colors and styles.

Hairy Faces

Men's moustaches and beards have come in and out of fashion over the centuries. Ancient Egyptian men were usually clean shaven, for example, although beards were fashionable from time to time.

Splitting hairs

In ancient Greece, in contrast, beards were common until the 5th century B.C.E., after which they were mainly worn only by old men and philosophers as a symbol of their freedom from worldly concerns. The Romans were obsessed with a clean shave. Viking men, on the other hand, wouldn't have be caught dead without a beard.

When beards and moustaches were in, men often experimented by altering their shape. For the noblemen of medieval Europe, for instance, a neatly trimmed and waxed forked beard was stylish for many decades.

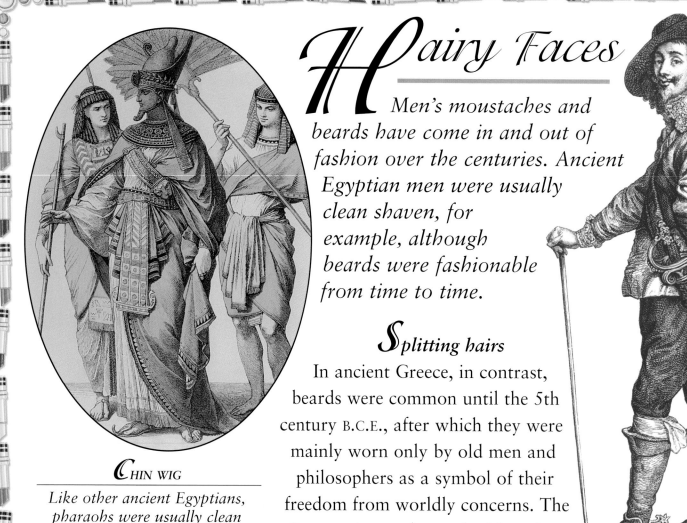

CHIN WIG

Like other ancient Egyptians, pharaohs were usually clean shaven. However, part of their royal regalia was a false beard tied around the chin with a strap.

MAKING A POINT

Upturned moustache tips and a goatee beard were all the rage in the first half of the 17th century.

VICTORIAN VALUES

As the 19th century progressed, luxuriant facial hair came to symbolize the Victorian ideals of seriousness and sobriety. The second man from the left wears sideburns, a new fashion.

A close shave

Men have often suffered for the sake of a smooth chin. For centuries, the only practical razor was a straight razor or cutthroat (a long blade with a handle), and shaving accidents were a daily hazard. The breakthrough in shaving technology came in 1901, when the American King C. Gillette (1855–1932) patented the first safety razor with a disposable blade. The final step toward facial freedom came in the 1920s, with the invention of the electric razor.

DESIGNER STUBBLE
In the 1980s film and pop icons such as singer George Michael (1963–) set a trend for the unshaven look.

LIP STYLE
A pencil-thin moustache became a must for men in the 1930s, after the style was sported by movie stars such as the swashbuckling Errol Flynn (right, 1909–1959) and the suave Clark Gable (1901–1960).

Natural Beauty

In the 1920s after centuries of pallor, the suntan became fashionable in Western society. The style guru Coco Chanel (1883–1971) is said to have inspired the change, when she accidentally became tanned after falling asleep in the sun.

Soaking up the sunshine

The risk of skin cancer from the sun's ultraviolet rays wasn't widely understood in those days, and for decades sunbathers focused on acquiring a tan as quickly as possible, not on protecting their skin. For those who couldn't afford vacations in hot countries, fake tans and sunlamps were soon being offered as alternatives.

SUNNY SIDE UP

Early sun lotions were designed to increase the chance of a tan or to soothe burned skin, not to protect it from the sun's ultraviolet rays.

FULL COVERAGE

Even at the beach, it was usual for the Victorian woman to cover every inch of her body with clothes and to carry a parasol to protect her fashionably pale complexion from the sun.

Staying in the shade

Effective sunscreen lotions became available in the late 1970s. By the 1990s health agencies were warning people to protect themselves from skin cancer by covering up, using sunscreens, and avoiding sunbathing. However, people continue to believe tans look healthy and attractive, so self-tanning lotions have become popular.

Fitness fanatics

The 20th century also saw a growing obsession with exercise. One of its earliest promoters was Molly Stack (1883– 1935), who in 1930 founded the Women's League of Health and Beauty with the aim of improving the health of the ordinary woman. Aerobics took off in the 1970s, and the fitness industry is now big business, with gyms offering everything from tai chi to aerobic classes.

Natural leader

In the 1970s Anita Roddick (1942–) pioneered, with great success, cosmetics made from natural, environmentally friendly ingredients.

The natural look

Supermodel Kate Moss (1974–) has been famous for her natural-looking makeup since the mid-1990s.

Let it burn

Today, millions of people are members of gyms or health and fitness clubs. They devote hours to exercise routines to shape and tone the body.

Mass Markets

When the first modern beauty parlors opened in the 19th and early 20th centuries, the focus was on skin care, not on makeup, which was only just becoming respectable. Two famous pioneers were Helena Rubenstein (1870–1965), who opened a salon in London in 1902, and Elizabeth Arden (1884–1966), who opened her first New York salon in 1909.

HOME BREWS

From ancient Egyptian times (right) until the 19th century, beauty tools and cosmetics were made by hand, often in people's homes.

Maxfactorize your own beauty

FOR THAT STAR-LIKE LOOK OF LOVELINESS

★ Share this glamour secret of Hollywood's most alluring screen stars, and *maxfactorize* your own beauty with famous *Max Factor Hollywood* Make-up in the correct shades which are individually prescribed to enliven, enhance, and harmonize perfectly with the natural colourings of your hair, eyes, and complexion. Try it . . . for a thrilling adventure in new beauty.

BETTY HUTTON
STAR OF PARAMOUNT'S
"DREAM GIRL"

COLOUR HARMONY MAKE·UP

created by
Max Factor
HOLLYWOOD

MAX FACTOR 'Cosmetics of the Stars' are obtainable from your local Chemist, Hairdresser & Store

From movies to mass production

Mass-produced makeup was a spin-off from the newly born film industry, and its founding father was Max Factor (1877–1938). Working in Hollywood in the 1910s, Factor started by concocting makeup that looked natural under the harsh lights of the movie camera. The success of these products led to his famous Pan-Cake brand makeup, which went on sale to the general public in the 1920s. Rubenstein and Arden followed rapidly with their own products.

STARS IN THEIR EYES

Max Factor became famous as makeup artist to the stars. One of his most successful advertising ploys was to use photos of well-known movie actresses to endorse his products.

Growth of an industry

Unlike the dangerous, lead-based cosmetics of earlier centuries, modern beauty products are formulated by scientists and subjected to rigorous safety tests before they are released on the market. Hundreds of ingredients are now used, including a cocktail of chemicals, natural dyes and oils, beeswax, petroleum, and talcum. Today, makeup is on sale virtually everywhere, from the supermarket to expensive department stores. Makeup artists undergo professional training, and the cosmetics industry is a multibillion-dollar business.

Movie magic

Makeup artists devised special masks to help transform actor John Hurt for the 1980 film The Elephant Man. *The quality of their work led to the establishment of a Best Makeup category in the 1981 Academy Awards, which was first won by* An American Werewolf in London.

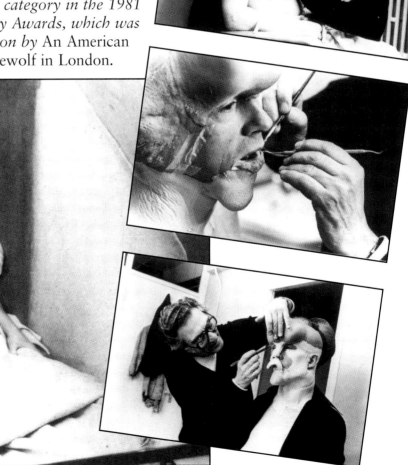

Timeline

Prehistory

Paintings on cave walls reveal that people were adorning their bodies with colored paints many thousands of years ago. Tattooing, scarring, piercing and other permanent forms of body art developed from body painting. Various forms of body art were practiced by different cultures worldwide. The earliest physical evidence of tattooing has been found on the 5,000-year-old body of Utzi the Iceman.

The ancient world

In the ancient civilizations that developed around the Mediterranean, the hot climate demanded relatively simple clothing that was complemented by elaborate makeup. In Egypt, the nobility used a range of homemade skin and hair care preparations, as well as tinted face, eye, and lip makeup. Greek and Roman women also used makeup, which included a face-paint made from poisonous white lead. The earliest known sets of false teeth were made in Italy about 700 B.C.E. by the Etruscans.

The Middle Ages

The Christian church preached against makeup, calling it devilry. The boldest women of nobility continued to use lip-paint and rouge discreetly. In France, women used wheat powder to whiten their faces. In South America, Mayan nobles inlaid their teeth with precious stones.

16th century

The Renaissance period saw a flowering of new ideas in art, architecture, and literature, and the beginnings of modern science. In the European royal courts, clothing and makeup became more intricate and sumptuous.

Noblewomen made up their faces heavily, coloring their eyes, lips, cheeks and even, sometimes, their teeth. White lead was used again as a face paint, and drops of deadly nightshade were used to expand the pupils.

17th century

Noblewomen continued applying their makeup liberally. Pale skin still set the nobility apart from the working classes, and symbolized aristocratic wealth and leisure. While the poor had rotten teeth extracted, the rich had theirs repaired with gold or lead fillings or replaced by false ones made of bone, ivory, or metal.

18th century

Heavy face makeup was worn by upper-class men as well as women, and white lead still formed the usual base for face cosmetics. Tiny black patches were used to cover up blemishes such as smallpox scars. Eyebrows were sometimes shaved off and replaced with false ones made of mouse skin. Captain James Cook's voyages introduced his sailors to Pacific tattooing practices, sparking a new interest in tattoos in the West.

19th century

A passion for simplicity swept Europe in the aftermath of the French Revolution (1789–1799) and extravagant makeup gave way to a more natural look. By the 1850s, obvious makeup was associated with actresses and prostitutes. Chalk and talcum had by now replaced white lead in cosmetic preparations.

20th century & beyond

As women began to gain new freedoms such as the right to vote, attitudes toward makeup became more liberal. Commercial lines of cosmetics began to be widely available in the 1920s, and suntans became fashionable. Red lips were the focal point of the face for several decades. In the 1960s cosmetics companies targeted a younger market, and heavily made-up eyes and pale lips became stylish. Makeup became sheerer in consistency and more light-reflective. In the last 25 years, there has been a renewed interest in body painting, tattooing, and piercing.

Glossary

body piercing making holes in the body to insert ornaments such as ear and nose rings

branding making an identifying mark, usually by burning it into the skin with a scalding hot iron tool. Cattle and criminals have been branded since ancient times.

cosmetics beauty products such as face makeup, which are designed to enhance appearance or provide skin care

cutthroat large blade with a handle, used for shaving

deadly nightshade poisonous plant used by the Elizabethans to make eyedrops that enlarged the pupils and caused the eyes to sparkle

goatee pointed beard resembling a goat's beard, and allowed to grow on the front of the chin only

henna reddish-orange dye obtained from the leaves of a shrub. In North Africa and Southeast Asia, henna has been used for centuries to color women's hair, hands, nails, and feet, as well as to dye mens' beards and horses' hooves and manes.

kohl black, lead-based eye makeup used by the ancient Egyptians

ochre type of mineral, red or yellow in color that has been ground up and used as a pigment since prehistoric times

plastic surgery branch of medicine concerned with the surgical repair or reshaping of the body. It is used not only to enhance beauty, but also to treat injuries such as burns. It can be extremely dangerous and expensive.

rouge cosmetic used to redden the cheeks, usually referred to today as blush

scarring body decoration practiced in many cultures, in which designs are cut into the skin to form permanent scars

sideburn line of hair allowed to grow down below the ears. Sideburns were named after General Ambrose E. Burnside (1824–1881), who popularized the style.

tattoo design or picture created by making thousands of tiny needle-pricks into the skin and allowing permanent dyes to seep into the holes

Index